Jersey Travel Guide

Sightseeing, Hotel, Restaurant & Shopping Highlights

Rachel Sharp

Table of Contents

Jersey

Jersey is the largest of the Channel Islands (after Guernsey, Sark and Alderney) and is a self-governing British crown dependency. The island, which lies off the northern coast of France is not a part of the United Kingdom nor is it a member of the European Union (although the free trade of goods from the EU is allowed). The official name of the island is the Bailiwick of Jersey and it is part of the ancient Duchy of Normandy. This idyllic island is well known for the Jersey Cow, the actress Lilly Langtry and the 1980s Bergerac television series.

Many thousands of years ago Jersey was once part of mainland France until a slab of mainly pink granite rock detached itself from the continent and settled some 14 miles off the coast. Discoveries on the island of Jersey have shown evidence of mankind dating back to the New Stone Age or 9,500 BC.

The history of Jersey has been shaped by many different people; Romans, Vikings, the Civil War, Napoleon and the German Occupation have all left their mark on the island.

The capital St Helier is named after the famous hermit and martyr from Jersey who was born in the 6th century. In the Royal Square in St Helier there is a statue of George II and it is from this point that all the distances on the island are measured. Along with the neighbouring Broad Street and King Street this is the heart of Jersey's shopping centre and a stone's throw from the harbour.

The terrain on the island varies from the long sandy beaches and pretty bays in the south to the more rugged cliffs in the north with the highest point above sea level a little less than 500 feet. With so much coastline it is no wonder that fresh fish is served just about everywhere. Spider crabs, John Dory, monkfish, scallops, mackerel, Dover sole and turbot are just a few.

Apart from holidays, Jersey is well-known for a couple of other things; Jersey Royal potatoes and Jersey cattle. Jersey Royal new potatoes are small but delicious and the sight of these in the shops heralds the beginning of spring. The beautiful brown Jersey cows are the only breed of cattle allowed on the island and they produce milk high in butterfat with the richest and creamiest taste ever.

Jersey fudge is hugely popular with tourists but a favourite snack on the island is Jersey Wonders or Mèrvelles. These twists of dough are deep fried and often found at village fêtes. According to tradition the Wonders should only be cooked when the tide is going out. If the tide is coming in the fat will spill over the edges of the pan!

Jersey uses the pound sterling as its currency and English and Scottish bank notes are legal tender. The island does have its own notes and coins with local designs on but while they are legal currency in the UK they are not legal tender. It would be up to a UK shopkeeper if he decided to accept them.

On the subject of money, in 2012 a hoard of golden coins were discovered in the parish of Grouville which are estimated to have a value of up to £10 million. There are thought to be 50,000 Celtic and Roman coins in the find.

The island also has its own semi-official national anthem which can be heard at Commonwealth Games and Island Games where there has to be a distinction between Jersey and UK teams. The semi-official song is called Ma Normandie and is also used as the regional anthem of Normandy. In light of this a competition was held to find a new anthem for Jersey and the winning song was called Island Home. It is likely that this will replace Ma Normandie.

English is spoken everywhere although until the end of the 19th century the language spoken in Jersey was Jêrrais with French used for official business. Now only about 3% of islanders speak their native language, mainly elderly people, although as with many dying languages there have been efforts to revive it in schools.

Culture

Jersey maybe small but it has more than its fair share of cultural gatherings and events. The Jersey Opera House in St Helier has something for all ages, with children's shows, ballet, opera, musicals, comedy and dance. The Jersey Arts Centre offers classic and contemporary performing arts, exhibitions, presentations, courses and workshops

There are many events and festivals held annually in Jersey but the Battle of Flowers is probably the most famous. The carnival has been held every year since 1902 when it was first staged in celebration of the Royal Coronation. Held in the middle of August it is now one of the largest floral carnivals in Europe and a highlight of the Jersey calendar. There is a daytime parade as well as a night time one and competitions for Mr and Miss Battle for teenagers and younger children. The Jersey Funfair and Food Village brings all the big rides to the island with stalls selling brightly coloured souvenirs and a variety of food tents.

The Battle of Britain air display held in September lasts for a week and in that time there are several static displays of aircraft and helicopters as well as a flying display. The Red Arrows, the RAF Falcons Parachute team and the Battle of Britain Memorial Flight take to the skies to thrill the watching crowds with their daring and skill.

The sporting event of the year in Jersey is the inter-island football match or Muratti. Cricket is very popular on Jersey and Guernsey and this leads to another nail-biting sports event each year between the islands.

Various cinemas have come and gone on the island since 1909 and the first talking picture was shown in 1929. Some 80 or so years later a ten screen multiplex shows the latest films in St Helier. For lovers of the silver screen every year there is the Jersey Film Festival with films shown outdoors on a giant screen. The Branchage Jersey International Film Festival held towards the end of September is attended by filmmakers from all over the world.

Location & Orientation

Jersey is in the Atlantic Ocean, more specifically in the Bay of Mont Saint-Michel. The island is about 100 miles south of Britain and a mere 14 miles from the French coast of Normandy. The island covers around 45 square miles and has a coastline of 48 miles with miles of sandy beaches, rocky outcrops and bunkers and other reminders of the Nazi Occupation in World War II.

The population of Jersey is about 98,000. Of these 34% live in the only town of St Helier. Half the inhabitants are true islanders and were born in Jersey, 31% were born elsewhere in the British Isles, 15% are Europeans and the remaining 4% from elsewhere in the world.

A lot of Jersey's economy centres on agriculture, tourism and finance. The island has always been duty free for luxury items but in 2008 a similar tax to VAT was introduced. Called GST or goods and services tax it is very low compared to the UK tax. Jersey has also been for many years a tax haven but this could be very shortly coming to an end.

To get to Jersey for business or pleasure most people fly into Jersey Airport. Jersey is connected to the other Channel Islands of Guernsey and Alderney as well as to the UK mainland and Europe by several airlines.

Travelling by bus on the island is easy. All routes radiate outwards from the Liberation Station in the capital of St Helier. There is a one day or three day bus pass which makes hopping on and off the buses simple.

Cycling is very popular and there is a very well signposted Cycle Network. Cyclists and pedestrians can use the traffic free route that goes from St Helier to Corbière passing by Jersey Airport. Cycle rental is available all over the island.

If you are taking your car to Jersey or planning on hiring one when you get there UK residents will be pleased to know that driving is on the left hand side. There is a strict 40mph speed limit throughout the whole island although it can be less in built up areas.

For anyone who prefers to travel by sea a high speed catamaran service operates between St Helier and Weymouth and Poole in the UK. For a slower crossing the combined passenger and freight ferry sails between Jersey and Portsmouth. There are also services between Jersey and St Malo in France.

There are no railways now on any of the islands although in the past there were limited services. All the lines have been dismantled and the only trains are miniature railways and the heritage steam railway.

Climate & When to Visit

The climate in Jersey is temperate with mild winters and cool summers. The Atlantic Ocean affects the climate with a cooling influence in the summer and a warming influence in the winter.

Spring in Jersey can be pleasant when all the flowers are coming into bloom and the promise of sunshine chases away the winter chills. Occasionally there can be a frost or two in March and April but by the time May comes the nights will at last be frost free. The daytime high can reach 15°C which in a sunny and sheltered spot can be rather nice. At night time the temperature dips down to 9°C. There is a fairly good chance of rain on half the days of each month, so don't travel without coats and umbrellas just yet.

The summer in Jersey is lovely and similar to the south coast of England but with more reliable sunshine. In August the beaches are busy as the daytime temperatures reach 20°C. In the evenings 11°C is still warm but maybe take a light wrap if you are planning on staying out late. It can still rain in the summer months but not too much and the driest month to plan a holiday is definitely July.

For anyone planning on splashing around in the Atlantic Ocean you will pleased to know that the Gulf Stream keeps the sea temperature at a reasonable 17°C in the summer months.

As the temperatures fall from the highs of 18°C in September and the leaves start to turn golden so the rain comes as well. September and October can be quite wet but November is the wettest month of the whole year. Along with the rain comes lows of 7°C and this can mean some frosty nights are round the corner. It is a time to dig out the scarves and gloves and think of steaming mugs of hot chocolate and roaring log fires.

January is the coldest month of the year in when temperatures at night can fall as low as 3°C. While thermals are not quite necessary it is wise to pack some cosy jumpers and warm socks. In the daytime the mercury will rise to 9°C and the frost will disappear for another day. Frost is likely in any of the winter months but the chances of a white Christmas or making a snowman are slight as snow very rarely falls in Jersey.

Sightseeing Highlights

Mont Orgueil Castle

St Martin
Jersey
JE3 6ET
Tel: +44 1534 853292
http://www.goreycastle.com/

Mont Orgueil Castle is often called Gorey Castle by English speakers and it sits on a mound overlooking Gorey Harbour. The castle dates from 1204 and was the first line of defence against marauders attacking the island. At the end of the 16th century Sir Walter Raleigh ordered the construction of Elizabeth Castle and Mont Orgueil fell out of favour.

The castle found a new purpose in life for a short time as a prison until a newer one was constructed in St Helier at the end of the 18th century. For a while troops were quartered at the castle until it became so dilapidated that it was abandoned in 1691 by both prisoners and troops.

A much needed grant has meant that in the 21st century Mont Orgueil can be visited safely by the public and previously unseen areas have been opened up. Parts of the castle have been renovated to provide visitor attractions such as the Prayer Nuts and Wheel of Urine!

Admission prices are £14 for adults, £7 for children and £10 for senior citizens.

Jersey War Tunnels

Les Charrières Malorey
St Lawrence
Jersey
JE3 1FU
Tel: +44 1534 860808
www.jerseywartunnels.com/

Hohlgangsanlage 8 or Ho8 is also known as the German Underground Hospital or Jersey War Tunnels.

This partially built hospital was built by the German occupying forces during World War II. There were just over 1,000 yards of tunnels completed and in that space there were 500 beds, gas-proof doors, operating theatres and a full heating and air-conditioning system.

After the liberation of the Channel Islands in 1945 the hospital was made into a visitor attraction detailing the occupation and as a memorial to the men who lost their lives digging the tunnels. Deep in the hillsides the tunnels tell their own stories of the war while the Garden of Reflection outside offers a breath of fresh air after the stark reality underground.

During the occupation the residents had the choice of going or staying; those who remained on the island fought and resisted the German soldiers, often unarmed, for five years. There is a lot of information to be taken in and not all of it is pleasant. Afterwards there is a Café and bar to enjoy some refreshments as well as shop with many gifts and books that cover the subject in great detail.

From March 1st until 31st October the Jersey War Tunnels are open from 10am to 6pm Monday to Sunday. The last entry is at 4.30pm. An adult pays £11.50, children pay £7.50 and senior citizens pay £10.50. This gives free entry to the Research Centre, War Trail and the Garden of Reflection.

La Hougue Bie Museum

La Route de la Hougue Bie
Jersey
JE2 7UA
Tel: +44 1534 853823

This historic site gets its name La Hougue Bie from the old Jèrriais/Norman language. Hougue means mound and underneath this 40 foot high mound is a long passage way. Excavated in 1925 fragments of vase were found as well as the remains of eight people. The site is one of the largest and most well-preserved passage graves or ceremonial sites of the Armorican Passage grave group covering the Channel Islands and Brittany.

The two chapels atop the mound are from the 12th and 16th centuries. During World War II the mound was used as a crucial lookout point and a command centre was built in the underground chamber. In the bunker now there is an exhibition in memory of the workers who were forced to help build the defences.

The museum on the site has many interesting artefacts and you can go right into the burial passage. The displays tell much about the geology and archaeology of Jersey. The grounds are well kept and a lovely place to take a picnic and spend the day. There are some super views from the top of the mound and on-site there are toilets and a tiny teashop.

Hougue Bie is open from 2nd April until 2nd November from 10am to 5pm. An adult pays £8, children pay £5 and senior citizens £7.

Durrell Wildlife Park

Les Augrès Manor
La Profonde Rue,
Trinity
Jersey
JE3 5BP
Tel: +44 1534 860000
www.durrell.org/

Gerald Durrell founded the Durrell Wildlife Conservation Trust over 50 years ago with the intention of saving endangered species. This park in Jersey is the headquarters of the Trust and in the 32 acres of beautifully kept parkland visitors can see 1400 reptiles, birds and mammals.

There is strong commitment to looking after the islands native species and large areas are devoted to these. There are opportunities to see increasingly rare species of birds as well as many carnivorous species in the Cloud Forest.

Durrell Wildlife Park is home to three generations of gorillas and these large primates are direct descendants of a very famous gorilla called Jambo. His story when you read it will make you change your way of thinking about these often misunderstood creatures.

If you need a break from all the beautiful and sometimes unusual animals Café Firefly serves delicious speciality sandwiches, giant salads and home grown Jersey jacket potatoes. In the Dodo Restaurant there is a selection of exciting and innovative Thai dishes to choose from.

The park is open from 9.30am to 5pm every day. An adult pays £14, children pay £10 and senior citizens £12.

Hamptonne Country Life Museum

Rue de la Patente
Jersey
JE3 1HS
Tel: +44 1534 863955

In the beautiful countryside of Jersey visitors to Hamptonne Country Life Museum are transported back a few hundred years. Demonstrations of life in the 17th century along with stories and traditions bring the era magically to life.

The outbuildings have been meticulously restored along with old farm implements and machinery and it is easy to imagine how hard life was before modern tools and mechanisation. There are nature trails to follow with lots of wildlife to see and an activity room for younger guests.

There are many traditional crafts on display throughout the season such as cabbage loaf baking, yarn spinning and lacemaking. The making of traditional cider is brought to life in the annual Fais'sie d'Cidre in October.

The museum is open from the end of May to the middle of September from 10am to 5pm daily. An adult pays £8, children pay £5 and senior citizens £7. There is a family ticket for two adults and two children priced at £24.

Living Legend Village

La Rue Du Petit Aleval
St.Peter
Jersey
JE3 7ET
Tel: +44 1534 485496
www.jerseyslivinglegend.co.je/

At the Jersey Living Legend Village visitors can discover all about the fascinating heritage of the island as well as have great fun in the nine acres of amusements and attractions. There are golf courses, a go-karting track, outdoor play areas and a full programme of live events and entertainment.

The spectacular Jersey Experience show recreates the story of Jersey and how history as well as time and nature have shaped the island. You can meet famous residents and learn about local legends and myths. The Battle of Jersey can be relived and you can see the reincarnation of St Helier. Experience what it was like when the Nazi forces occupied the island and how the inhabitants felt when they were finally liberated.

This is a very large adventure and leisure village and there is enough to the whole family occupied all day along with several cafés, a restaurant and a crêperie.

The park is open seven days a week from April to October 9.30am to 5pm and five days a week from March to November 9.30am to 5pm, closed Thursdays and Fridays.

Entry into the Living Legend Village is free but there are charges for the golf, go-karting and Jersey Experience. All the information is on the website.

Elizabeth Castle

St Aubin's Bay, St Helier, Jersey, JE3 3NU
Tel: +44 1534 723 971

When the stronghold of Mont Orgueil was unable to withstand the attacks from ships the construction of the new castle was ordered. Built in the 16th century and named after Elizabeth 1st it is now the site of a museum that displays several centuries of military and regimental memorabilia.

Every Sunday when the castle is open a team of enthusiasts give displays of what life was like then accompanied by muskets firing and the roaring of cannons. On the Sunday closest to the 16th July, St Helier's Day, an open air service is held at the castle.

Elizabeth Castle is situated on L'Islet, a small island that lies in St. Aubins Bay. As the island gets cut off by the tide there are two small wading vehicles that ferry visitors across or at low tide it is possible to walk across the causeway.

The castle is open from early April to early November from 10am to 5.30pm. Admission to the castle is £10 for adults and children and senior citizens pay £7. A family pass can be purchased for £31. For an extra £3 per person a combined ferry and castle ticket can be purchased.

Jersey Sea Safaris

Oyster Bay
La Grande Mielle,
Fauvic
Grouville
Jersey
JE3 9BN.
Tel: +44 7829 772222
www.jerseyseafaris.com/

Jersey has a magnificent shoreline and there no better way to see it than from a boat trip around the island.

There are regular boat trips as well as ferry rides across to France just 30 minutes away.

There are trips out to Les Ecrehous as well which is a rocky outcrop and an internationally important area for wildlife and wetlands.

The Minquiers Safari takes you on a 25 minute ride from Jersey but you might be forgiven if you think you have been transported much further afield. This group of tiny islands varies widely with the tides but the clear blue water and white sandy beaches stay the same. There is always a chance of seeing dolphins as well as seals and a wide array of birdlife.

The price for the trip to Les Ecrehous is £39 for adults and £30 for children and the duration is two hours. All the trips are clearly priced on the website.

St Brelade's Bay & Fisherman's Chapel

La Route de la Baie
St Brelade
Jersey
JE3 8EF

A visit to Jersey would not be complete without spending some time at St Brelade's Bay and visiting the Fisherman's Chapel. The chapel was built from crushed limpet shells and is a very pretty place to sit and admire the views across the bay as well as the stunning sunsets.

St Brelade's Bay is Jersey's busiest beach with wide expanses of golden sands, edged with neat green lawns, palm trees and well-kept flower beds. The bay faces south and is very sheltered from the Atlantic Ocean making it a paradise for sun worshippers.

There are plenty of toilets and other facilities scattered along the shore line as well as a variety of water sports from pedalo's to beach volleyball and trampolines.

Channel Islands Military Museum

La Grande Route Des Mielles
St Ouen
Jersey
JE3 2FN
Phone: +44 1534 483205
www.cimilitarymuseum.co.uk/

The Channel Islands Military Museum is in a large bunker and was one of over 60 similar sites that the Nazi's constructed to defend St. Ouens Bay. The underground rooms are full of artefacts and other memorabilia from the years of the occupation. There are models in uniforms and several small vehicles as well as sound bites from the era.

From the outside the museum doesn't look as if it very big, but is rather like the Tardis with many rooms inside. A lot of the items are personal stuff that the Germans left behind and it makes you realise just what it must have been like living on the island through the war. The museum is privately owned and many of the stories on display are from local people who lived through the terrible times.

The museum is open from April to October from 10am to 5pm. Admission prices are £4 for adults and £2 for children.

aMaizin! Adventure Park & Maze

La Hougue Farm
La Grande Route de St Pierre
St Peter
Jersey
JE3 7AX
Tel. +44 1534 482116
www.jerseyleisure.co.uk/

This fantastic adventure park offers fun and entertainment all day long for everyone. The entry price includes all the rides, events, displays and activity sessions. In the Barnyard there are cute and furry animals to cuddle while for some adrenalin filled adventure the three go-kart tracks are suitable for all ages. There are tractor rides, a huge 50ft Jumping Pillow plus Water Warriors, Bouncy Hoppers, football, games with hula hoops, games with boats and games with hammocks.

Every July a huge maze is created from the cereal crop and a scavenger hunt is included in the admission price. The 40ft long Towering Toboggan Run is great fun for all ages while in the Dusty Mountain Goldmine you can try your hand at searching for treasure.

At the Snack Shack you can get a decent meal and there are plenty of places for parents to enjoy a coffee or ice cream while younger family members play safely nearby. A shop on site sells many unusual and quirky gifts and is very popular with locals as well as visitors.

The park is open daily from March/April to September from 10am to 6pm. An adult ticket costs just over £8, children aged four and over pay £8.50. For senior citizens and children aged between 2 and 3 years the cost is £6.50. Children under two get in free and groups of four or people pay £8 per person.

St Ouen's Bay

St Ouen is in the north-west corner of Jersey and is one of the twelve parishes of the island. The beach here is known as "Five Mile Beach" as it stretches into the distance offering mile upon mile of flat almost white sand for relaxing on. If you want a day away from the more popular spots this is definitely the place to head for. The views reach across the Atlantic Ocean to La Rocco Tower and Corbière and the lighthouse.

The area is popular with surfers and those that enjoy beach activities but there is plenty of room for everyone. There are beach bars and kiosks all the way along the bay. Some have BBQ's and you can take your plate of food and sit on the warm golden sand.

There are car parks as well as roadside parking all the way along the bay. In the summer months the beaches are patrolled by lifeguards. There is plenty to explore with rock pools, dunes and fortifications and gun batteries to remind visitors of less peaceful times.

Recommendations for the Budget Traveller

Places to Stay

Jersey Accommodation & Activity Centre (JAAC)

La Rue de La Pouclee et des Quatre Chemins
Faldouet St Martin
Jersey
JE3 6DU
Tel: +44 1534 498636
www.jerseyhostel.co.uk/

This is a great place on the island with sensibly priced accommodation and excellent facilities. There are dorms for big groups and a choice of smaller rooms for singles, couples and families. Large groups can occupy a whole wing with separate accommodation for supervisory staff.

JAAC is a short stroll from Mont Orgueil Castle and the harbour, with the Durrell Wildlife Park 10 minutes away by car. There are buses from the nearby stop that leave every 20 minutes for St Helier.

There is a selection of single, double, twin, treble and quad bedded rooms, many with ensuite facilities. A light continental breakfast is included but there are many meal plans on offer including packed lunches for days out exploring.

The hostel is in a large old building but there is nothing antiquated about the rooms or service. The sheets and towels are provided and there is a communal games room, laundry and self-catering kitchen. With plenty of outside space for relaxing this is an ideal budget friendly location for a holiday in Jersey.

JAAC is open all year round and the reception hours are 9am to 1pm and 5pm to 9pm. There are often events held at the centre such as craft fairs and dog shows and team building activities can be organised for companies.

Mornington Hotel

Don Road
St Helier
Jersey
JE2 4QD
Tel: +44 1534 724452
www.morningtonhoteljersey.com/

For over 50 years this family run hotel has offered an excellent standard of accommodation a short stroll from the centre of St Helier. The beach at Havre des Pas and the pretty gardens of Howard David Park are just around the corner.

All the bedrooms are ensuite with central heating and a hospitality tray and have flat screen TV with English, Spanish, French, Italian and German channels. There is free Wifi throughout the building. For a touch of romance there are some four poster "honeymoon" rooms available as well.

There are single, twin, double and family rooms to choose from and the rates start from a very reasonable £45 per room per night for two people sharing. The price includes a substantial continental breakfast served in the pretty dining room. Special diets can be catered for on request.

In bar and lounge areas guests can enjoy some friendly chat with the staff or relax and watch TV. There is a quiet area as well with a selection of books and newspapers to choose from.

Olanda Guest House

La Rue du Croquet
St Aubin
Jersey
JE3 8BZ
Tel: +44 1534 742573
www.olandaguesthouse.com

The Olanda is between St Helier and St Brelade so is an ideal location for a base on this beautiful island. Situated in the high street everything is in within a very short walk; shops, bars and restaurants are all close by and of course the wonderful beaches and glittering sea are not far away either.

This pretty guest house in the fishing village of St Aubin is family run and is very popular with families. The eleven guest rooms are all bright and spacious with colour TV, hairdryer and a hospitality tray. The ground floor rooms all have doors leading out to the garden and patio. The rooms are all double or twin bedded and there are two family rooms with double beds and interconnecting rooms with bunks beds.

The price per person per night is from £25 and this includes a choice of a Continental breakfast or a hearty full English breakfast with vegetarian options available. There is a bar just for residents on the patio which is safely enclosed and traffic free. There is free Wifi and some private car parking.

Undercliff Guest House

Bouley Bay
Jersey
JE3 5AS
Tel: +44 1534 863058
www.undercliffjersey.com/

The Undercliff is in a beautiful countryside setting to the north of the island of Jersey. It is a super place for a peaceful and relaxing holiday with the sea and pretty harbour 200 yards away and open countryside the other. For diving enthusiasts the clear and warm seas of Bouley Bay offer great opportunities for checking out the world under the waves.

There is a choice of accommodation only, self-catering or bed and breakfast in this 4 star rated complex. There are 12 rooms and as the building they are in is over 200 years old they all vary in shape and size, which adds to the character.

There is nothing out-dated about the facilities and the ensuite rooms are all comfortably furnished with hospitality trays, TV and free Wifi included. Some of the ground floor rooms have sea views.

There are pretty gardens and a sun terrace for guests to use and heated swimming pool in the main season of May to September. From the terrace there are views across to the French coast depending on the weather.

There are twin, double, treble or family rooms to choose from and the prices start from £25 per person per night. This includes a full English breakfast. For guests wishing to be more independent there is a one bedroom apartment or two, three bedroom villas to choose from.

Rocqueberg View

Rue de Samares, St Clement, Jersey, JE2 6LS
Tel: +44 1534 852642
www.rocquebergview.co.uk/

For anyone that loves gardening or just likes to see beautiful flowers this is a super place to stay. Rocqueberg View is a winner of the St Clement garden competition and it is easy to see why.

Stunning and colourful displays cascade from every windowsill and fill every corner and flowerbed.

The guest house is the most southerly in the British Isles and is a couple of hundred yards from the excellent Green Island beach where the white sand gently slopes down to meet the sparkling blue sea. There is a heated pool in the pretty garden which is ideal for a quick dip under the warm Jersey sunshine. In the guest lounge there are books and magazines for a peaceful and relaxing break from seeing the sights.

There is so much here within such a short distance that guests will never be short of places to go, whether it is shopping, eating and drinking or looking for entertainment or culture. Despite its peaceful location Rocqueberg View is only a couple of miles from the bustling town of St Helier.

The double, twin or family rooms are all ensuite with a hospitality tray, TV and hairdryer. A decent breakfast is included and for families there are cots, high chairs and babysitting available.

Prices start from £25 per person per night.

Places to Eat & Drink

Big Verns

La Grande Route des Mielles
St Ouen's Bay
St Peter
Jersey
JE3 7FN
Tel: +44 1534 481705

Head over to the west of Jersey and find Big Vern's as for the perfect meal by the beach this is a great choice. The large restaurant has a big terrace where diners can soak up the sun while tucking into the delicious food. There is lots of free car parking as well.

Breakfast is one of the specialities but if you arrive a little later there is sizzling tuna, grilled sardines or homemade steak and kidney pie. There is a good choice of vegetarian foods and they are family friendly.

If you like walking take a gentle stroll over the cliffs from Plemont and end up at Big Vern's for a reviving pint, it is the only restaurant on this beautiful stretch of sand and well worth the effort.

Big Vern's is open every day from 9am to 6pm with later closing from April to October at 9pm.

Parade Cafe

17 The Parade
St Helier
Jersey
JE2 3QP
Tel: +44 1534616827

This family owned café has been serving up good quality and reasonably priced meals in Jersey for many years. It is a few steps away from the lively and bustling high street and offers a variety of light meals as well as sandwiches and cakes.

If you fancy afternoon tea there are always plenty of delicious homemade cakes on offer and a mouth-watering choice of freshly cooked pancakes. The Parade Café is bright and welcoming with a small terrace for guests to enjoy the sunshine while they dine.

Maria and Joe welcome diners Monday to Saturday 7.30am to 7pm and on Sunday from 9am to 4pm.

BreakWater Café

La Route de St Catherine, St Martin, Jersey, JE3 6DD
Tel: +44 1534 851141

With stunning views of St. Catherine's Bay this café is a super place for dining al fresco on the beautiful island of Jersey. There are many walkways and pretty paths just waiting to be explored close by before or after your meal.

The menu uses local ingredients where possible and there are healthy options as well as vegetarian meals. The very popular Jersey cream tea is one of the specialities served with thick yellow cream from Jersey's own cows.

The BreakWater Café is open Monday to Sunday from 9am to 6pm although they do stop serving hot food at 5pm.

Wayside Café

Mont Sohier
St Brelade
Jersey
JE3 8EA
Tel: +44 1534 743915

Down on the south side of Jersey is St Brelade's Bay and this is where you can find the family friendly Wayside Café. The picture postcard perfect views of the bay from the outside terrace could easily be an advert for a tourism poster.

The sun bleached tables and wooden decking are fine for sitting at straight from the beach, no worry about shoes and washing the sand off your feet here. The food is great with all the classic dishes anyone could want served with a smile in a beautiful setting. The homemade cakes are amazing and what could be better than a freshly made milkshake on a warm day backing in the sun.

Wayside Café is open from 9am to 8.45 pm seven days a week although they close slightly earlier on Wednesday at 5pm. It is a great place for children and man's best friend is welcome outside.

Café Poste

La Rue de la ville es Renauds GB
Grouville
Jersey
JE3 9FY
Tel: +44 1534 859696
www.cafeposte.co.uk/

This old post office and former railway station has been turned into a rustic and welcoming café. There is a collection of curios to admire while waiting for your meal and a definite French ambience. It is a small and cosy place for a light lunch, a romantic meal or a group of friends to get together and enjoy carefully prepared local foods.

There is a wide choice of fish from the local daily catch as well as tender steaks cooked to perfection. A daily set menu has a mouth-watering selection of choices and there is a good selection of vegetarian options and special diets can be catered for.

Café Poste is open Wednesday to Sunday from 11.45am to 2pm and 6.30pm to 9pm. On Saturday and Sunday they open slightly earlier for breakfast service from 9.30.

Places to Shop

Central Market, St Helier

The market isn't the biggest in the world but it will give you a taste of everything is that is great about this wonderful island. The market hall is in the centre of St Helier and opened in 1882. The Victorian building is worth visiting just for its architectural splendour and the recently restored fountain.

There are plenty of goldfish in the fountain and children are encouraged to throw coins in. Once a month the fountain is emptied and the money given to local charities.

There is a wide choice of fresh produce all grown in the rich Jersey soil. Antiques, jewellery, flowers and clothes of which many have a French feel are all readily available. Don't miss the Red Triangle Stores; it is rather like stepping into a time-warp of 100 years ago.

The market is open 7.30am to 5.30pm Monday to Saturday but does close early on a Thursday afternoon.

Farm & Craft Market

St Brelade Parish Hall
St Aubin
Jersey
JE3 8BS
Tel: +44 1534 853395

On alternate Saturdays from March to October in St Aubin there is the local craft market. Set up along the harbour side the stall holders vie for your attention with their homemade and handcrafted displays.

Everything will have been grown, pickled, processed, baked or smoked by the stall holder who will be only too delighted to explain the process and let you try some samples.

The market is open from 9am to 2pm.

Jersey Pottery

Halkett Place, St Helier, Jersey, JE2 4WG
Tel: +44 1534 850815
www.jerseypottery.com/

Jersey Pottery is one of the oldest businesses on the island. From a small family business that started in 1946 the distinctive pottery is now sold in 20 countries throughout the world. The business is run today by the grandsons of the founders, Clive and Jesse Jones.

The shop at Halkett Place is the perfect place to buy an original piece of Jersey Pottery to take home as a keepsake. There is a wide selection of items from small gifts and mementoes to quality cookware and furnishings.

The ceramics, many with fishy designs, grace the shelves of shops like Fortnum & Mason and Harrods. A visit to the town shop in St Helier gives the chance to buy your own piece of pottery and they are open Monday to Saturday 9.30am to 5.30pm.

Jersey Lavender Farm

Rue du Pont Marquet
St Brelade
Jersey
JE3 8DS
Tel: +44 1534 742933
www.jerseylavender.co.uk/

The nine acres of lavender ripen under the warm sun and then they are harvested and distilled into pure lavender oil. The oil is used in a range of fragrances and products and is a natural and therapeutic ingredient. The farm was started in 1983 and is run today by the son of the people that started it.

Everybody loves the delicate perfume of lavender and there is wealth of gifts and practical accessories to choose from at the Lavender Farm. With everything from candles to cologne there is bound to be something you want.

Through the summer there are short tours of the lavender distillery with the chance to smell many of the different oils they produce. Once you have admired the sea of purple stretching in all directions the Sprigs Café serves the most delicious lavender scones with heaps of thick, rich Jersey cream.

The lavender farm, shop and café are open from April to September from 10am to 5pm Tuesday to Sunday. There are details on the website of the different tours and talks about lavender.

De Gruchy

46-52 King Street
St Helier
Jersey
JE4 8NN
Tel: +44 1534 818818
www.degruchys.com/

For over 200 years the de Gruchy store has been an essential part of the St Helier shopping scene. It is one of the oldest department stores in the United Kingdom and with 76,000 square feet of shopping space it is in a prime location in the main shopping area.
Behind the smart creamy-white façade the vast open floors have sections for men, women, children, travel, beauty and household.

The Brasserie at de Gruchy is great for a bite to eat as a respite from shopping. Everything is freshly made in the store and there is a full lunch menu as well as sandwiches and cakes.

The store is open from 9am to 6pm Monday to Saturday and closed on Sundays.

CPSIA information can be obtained at www.ICGtesting.com
Printed in the USA
LVOW01s1828250515

439755LV00039B/1839/P

9 781505 577488